PATHFINDERS
IN EXPLORATION

Exploring Deserts

EDITORIAL PLANNING
AMR

M
MACMILLAN

First published 1987

Published by
MACMILLAN EDUCATION LTD
Houndmills, Basingstoke, Hampshire RG21 2XS
and London
Companies and representatives
throughout the world

Authors: Derek Cullen and John Murray-Robertson

Designed and typeset by The Pen and Ink Book Company Ltd, London

Illustrated by Eugene Fleurey

Picture research by Faith Perkins

Printed in Hong Kong

British Library Cataloguing in Publication Data

Exploring deserts - (Pathfinders in
  exploration).
  1. Discoveries (in geography) – Juvenile
  literature   2. Deserts – Juvenile literature
  I. Series
  910'.09154   G175

ISBN 0-333-43947-3
ISBN 0-333-43953-8 Set

Photographic Credits

t=top b=bottom l=left r=right

The author and publishers wish to acknowledge, with thanks, the following photographic sources: 28*t* J Allan Cash, London; 39 Barnaby's Picture Library, London; 15, 26-27, 36*l* BBC Hulton Picture Library, London; 38 Bettmann Archive, New York; 10, 13, 17*b*, 18*l* and *r* (courtesy of Lady Anne Lytton and the British Library), 36*r*, 40*t* BPCC/Aldus Archive, London; 11*t*, 28-29 Bridgeman Art Library, London; 25*l* (Stein Collection) The British Library, London; 42 Church of Jesus Christ of Latter Day Saints; 23 (photograph Marcus Brooke), 34 (photograph Penny Tweedie) Colorific, London; 22*t* Courtesy of Curtis Brown; contents 11*b*, 33*t* Mary Evans Picture Library, London; 25*r* (reproduced from Buddist Cave Paintings by Basil Gray) Courtesy of Faber and Faber; 12 (portrait of Alexandrine Tinné by H A d'Ainecey) Haags Gemeentenemuseum, The Hague; 8, 14 Sonia Halliday Photographs; 8-9, 17*t*, 41, 43 Robert Harding Photographs, London; 6 Michael Holford; 26-27 John Massey Stewart; 5*r*, 7, 29, 31, 32, 33*b*, 35*t* and *b*, 40*b* Peter Newark's Western Americana; title 51*l*, 37 Picturepoint (UK); 16-17, 20*b*, 21, 22*b* Royal Geographical Society, London; 20*t* John Topham Picture Library

Cover photograph courtesy of Picturepoint (UK).

The publishers have made every effort to trace the copyright holders, but if they have inadvertently overlooked any, they will be pleased to make the necessary arrangement at the first opportunity.

Note to the reader
In this book there are some words in the text which are printed in **bold** type. This shows that the word is listed in the glossary on page 46. The glossary gives a brief explanation of words which may be new to you.

Contents

Introduction

In this book, we are going to look at some of the people who risked their lives in the dry, lands we call **deserts**. Deserts are the areas of the world where there is little or no rainfall year after year. There are places in some deserts where it has not rained for years. Deserts are **barren**. Very few plants or trees can survive there because water is so scarce. Hardly any animals can live where there is so little to eat or drink.

There are different types of deserts. There are rocky deserts like the Great Basin Desert in the United States. Some deserts are sandy like the Arabian Desert.

▼ These are the main desert regions of the world. Deserts cover about one-seventh of the land surface of the Earth. Only about five per cent of the Earth's population live in deserts.

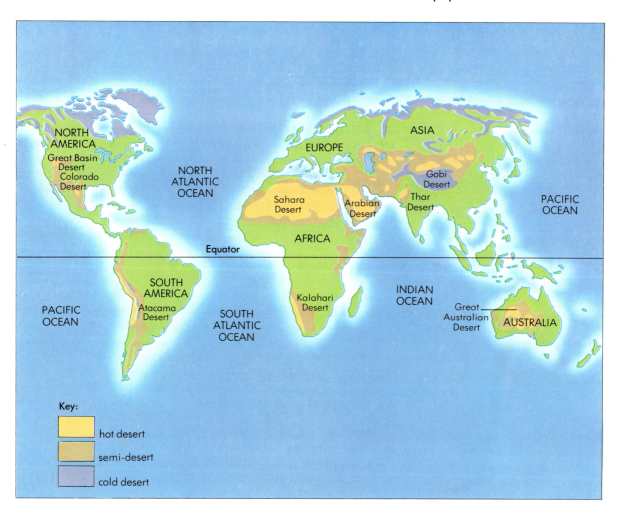

Key:
- hot desert
- semi-desert
- cold desert

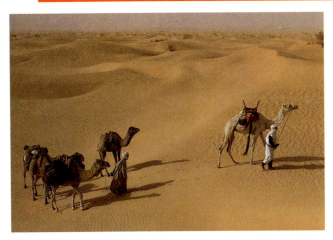

▲ These desert people are travelling through the Sahara Desert in Algeria. Camels have been used for hundreds of years to carry people and food from one oasis to another.

Desert people

Most of the people who live in the deserts of the world do not spend very much time in one place. They are called **nomads**. These people always move from place to place in order to find food for themselves and their animals. They travel from one water-hole to another. These water-holes are called **oases**. Sometimes, there is enough water at an oasis for people to live there all the time.

Why explore deserts?

Over the years, people have been drawn to the deserts for many reasons. Some early explorers were **traders**. They hoped to set up safe ways, or **routes**, across the deserts. These routes took them to the lands where they bought gold, spices, salt and other goods. Many of the early explorers wanted to draw maps to show the oases, the mountains and other landmarks. Sometimes, they just hoped to gain honour and fame for themselves and for their countries. Then, there were explorers who went to make their fortunes. They looked for **treasure**, like diamonds and precious metals, in the deserts.

Not all explorers were looking for profit or fame. Some were drawn to the danger and mystery of the desert. One explorer, called Wilfred Thesiger, explored the Arabian Desert about 40 years ago. He was often tired and thirsty, but he said he loved the freedom and way of life of the desert. He is like many explorers in this book. These people look for lonely places to test themselves. They want to go into the unknown, even if they risk death by doing so.

▼ Francisco Coronado was an early Spanish explorer. In 1540, he set out to find gold and other riches, but instead found Indian villages in parts of south west America. Coronado explored the Rio Grande and central Kansas.

The Sahara Desert

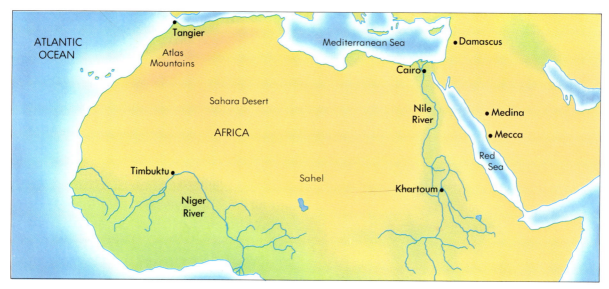

The largest desert in the world is the Sahara in North Africa. A lot of the Sahara is rocky sandstone land with high mountain tops, or **peaks**. Some of the peaks are covered in snow. In other parts, there are thousands of kilometres of white sand. The Sahara is very hot. The average daytime **temperature** is 38 °C.

Until recently, only nomads and traders travelled in the Sahara. The traders took goods from country to country. They travelled in groups for safety, going from oasis to oasis. They took camels with them to carry their goods. Some groups of traders still travel like this today. These groups are called **caravans**.

Other people cross the desert more quickly and easily in trucks. These trucks are built to travel on rough ground.

▲ The Sahara Desert stretches across northern Africa from the Atlantic Ocean in the west to the Red Sea in the east. In the north, it goes from the Atlas Mountains to the Sahel region in the south. It covers parts of ten different countries.

Ibn Battuta

It was not an easy journey when Ibn Battuta went on his travels in 1325. This rich Arab from Tangier in Morocco was a good **Muslim**. He wanted to follow his religion's rule. This rule says that Muslims should visit the holy cities of **Islam**, called Mecca and Medina. His first journey took him straight across the Sahara, and on to Damascus, in Syria. There, he got married. Then, he went on to Mecca alone. He wrote about these journeys in his travel book *The Rihlah*.

The great traveller

Battuta is known as 'the great traveller of Islam'. He went to many cities and even reached China. He also spent some time in East Africa. For two years, he lived on the Maldive Islands, in the Indian Ocean. He covered 120 000 km on his many journeys. People say he met 60 different rulers on his travels. He tried 'never to travel the same road a second time'.

The journey to Timbuktu

Battuta's last and most famous journey was across the Sahara. He went from Tangier to West Africa and back. He wanted to follow the traders' route. Battuta wrote, 'There is no road . . . nothing but sand blown by the wind'.

▲ Ibn Battuta travelled all over North Africa. He also went as far as China on one of his journeys.

◀ This picture of a caravan of Muslim pilgrims was painted over 750 years ago. They are travelling together on camels and horses on a religious journey. They may be going to the holy cities of Mecca and Medina.

Once, he was ten days from the nearest water. Somehow, he managed to reach a village. The people in the village were slaves who worked for the salt traders. All their houses were built of salt.

At last, Battuta reached Timbuktu, a town in the south of the Sahara Desert. Many people still go there to trade. From there, he went down part of the Niger River in a canoe. After more journeys in the area around Timbuktu, he went back across the Sahara to Tangier.

Battuta died in Tangier after 30 years of desert travel. He had used no maps on his journeys. He found his way using the Sun and stars, and by talking to nomads who knew about the desert.

The first explorers

The North Africans knew about the routes through the desert before maps were drawn. People have lived in the Sahara for many thousands of years. Some live in small towns built near the oases. They grow dates and **millet**, a type of grain, and they keep goats. The other people of the Sahara are nomads. They belong to the Beduoin and Tuareg people. Their camel caravans cross the desert with the nomads' tents and all their food and clothing. The nomads trade in gold, dates, and meat **preserved** with salt. They also trade in **saltpetre**, which is used to make gunpowder.

▲ An oasis in Saudi Arabia where water is plentiful. A town has been built and crops are being grown. Oases have been centres of trade for hundreds of years.

▲ These camels are carrying salt which is an important trade item for desert nomads. The traders and their camels cross the desert in a long caravan.

The Europeans did not find ways of crossing the Sahara until about 200 years ago. They traded for gold with the Africans on the west coast. They heard tales of splendid kingdoms inland, which were supposed to be filled with gold and precious jewels. The Europeans wanted to find these kingdoms and their treasures.

The Europeans also traded in gold, silver and slaves on the east coast of Africa. They wanted to find an overland route from west to east. This was to avoid the sea route around the Horn of Africa. Pirates often attacked ships in these waters.

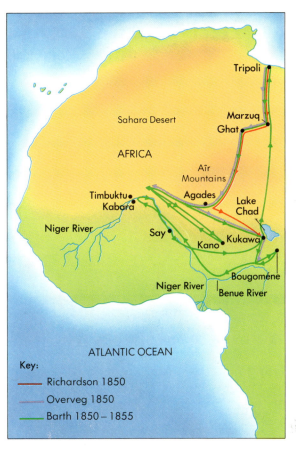

▲ The routes followed by James Richardson, Heinrich Barth and Adolf Overveg.

The unknown continent

Early maps show how little the Europeans knew about Africa. Traders from Europe knew of a way inland from the west coast to Timbuktu and Lake Chad. However, about 200 years ago, people in Europe wanted to draw better maps. They also wanted to study Africa in order to get to know more about the rivers, the mountains, and the peoples of Africa. Some people set up **expeditions**. They sent out groups of people to find out more about this land, or **continent**.

Expedition to the Niger River

One of these expeditions was set up in Britain and led by James Richardson. His aim was to find out about the area, or **region**, around the upper part of the Niger River. This region is on the south west edge of the Sahara. Richardson wanted to map the cities and caravan routes in the area.

At this time, people could not go all the way up the Niger River to Lake Chad and Timbuktu. This was because they did not know where the mouth of the Niger was. So Richardson decided to cross the Sahara from the north. In 1850, he set off for Timbuktu with boxes of goods, or **supplies**, loaded on to camels. He even took a boat which was in two halves. He was going to use it to sail on Lake Chad!

9

Richardson's expedition

Richardson picked the people for his journey very carefully. He chose two Germans to go with him. One was called Adolf Overveg, and the other was called Heinrich Barth. Barth had studied geography, and could also speak Arabic well.

South to Lake Chad

In 1850, the group left Tripoli for Lake Chad. They travelled to Marzuq and Ghat, two oasis towns in the heart of the Sahara Desert. From there, they went across the Aîr Mountains to Agades. They were in constant danger from the Tuareg people, who often stopped them to ask for money. Barth also found it hard to get on with Richardson. They had many arguments.

When the group reached Agades, they split up. Richardson went south east to Kukawa. Barth and Overveg went west to map the area east of Timbuktu.

Barth often went off to explore places on his own. Once, he went by himself to find the city of Kano, now a part of Nigeria. He dressed in Arab clothes and dyed his face. He did this so he could more easily get around among the local people. Barth liked the city of Kano. There were about 30 000 people living there at that time. He found out a lot about the people, and came to respect their way of life.

Barth rejoined Overveg, and they went off to Kukawa to find Richardson. When they reached Kukawa, they found that Richardson had died of a fever. The two Germans then set out to explore the area south of Lake Chad. They travelled as far as the Benue River, which flows into the Niger River. Both men spent 15 months in this area. While they were there, Barth set off once again on his own. He went to the city of Bougoméne south of Lake Chad. There, the local ruler put him in prison for a short time. When he was released, Barth rejoined his friend. Sadly, Overveg also died of a fever a few weeks later.

◀ A water-hole in the Sahara Desert. The lives of desert explorers depended on oases and water-holes. If a water-hole went dry, the explorers could die of thirst.

Barth alone

Barth was now alone. In November 1852, he set off on a long journey west to Timbuktu. It took him ten months to get there. As he went along, he made notes of the things he saw and the people he met. At last, he reached Timbuktu. He found it a rich and busy trading city. The houses were made of brick rather than mud. This showed that Timbuktu was a wealthy place.

Barth spent another two and a half years in West Africa. Then, in May 1855, he decided to return home. He left Lake Chad and went back across the Sahara Desert to Tripoli. On his return to Germany, he gave advice to many other expeditions. His maps were the best that people in Europe had ever seen of West Africa.

▲ This picture of Kano has been drawn from one of the sketches Heinrich Barth made on his expedition to West Africa.

▲ This is a painting of Heinrich Barth reaching Timbuktu. Timbuktu is in the south west of the Sahara. Timbuktu used to be an important centre on the trans-Saharan caravan route.

Alexandrine Tinné

After Barth's return to Europe, a Dutch woman set out for North Africa. She was called Alexandrine Tinné. Like Barth and Richardson, she wanted to find out all about the Sahara and its people.

Alexandrine Tinné came from a wealthy family in the Netherlands. She could speak many languages, including Arabic. This was very useful on her journeys in North Africa. She could also ride horses well.

The first journey

In 1863, Tinné set out for Cairo in Egypt with a group of people. Her mother, her aunt and six scientists were in the group. First, they sailed up the Nile River to Khartoum. They hoped to explore the area around one of the smaller rivers which flows into the Nile. This river is called the Bahr-al-Ghazal.

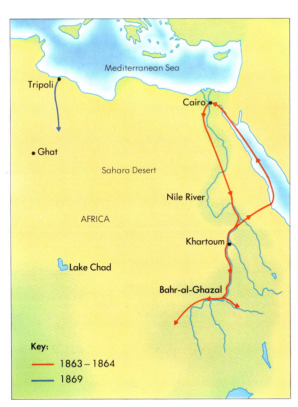

▲ The routes Alexandrine Tinné and her companions took on their travels in the Sahara Desert.

▲ This is a portrait of Alexandrine Tinné. She was very adventurous and in her twenties when she went to Africa.

The journey was both hard and unhappy for Tinné. Both her mother and one of the scientists died of a fever. Another one of the scientists was killed by a buffalo. After these sad events, the rest of the group decided it would be best for them to return to Khartoum. They had been back in Khartoum only a few days when Tinné's aunt also died of fever.

Tinné did not want to give up. She was a brave woman. She decided to return to Cairo. There she set up a **base**, from which she went on journeys to the western Sahara.

Final journey

In 1869, Tinné went to Tripoli in Libya. There, she joined a caravan which was crossing the Sahara to Lake Chad. The area they were to cross was controlled by the Tuareg people. Tinné hired two Dutch sailors to act as her bodyguards.

The Tuareg people thought that Europeans were their enemies. They often forced them to gave up their goods and their money. This made it hard for any group of people to cross the Sahara in safety.

When the caravan was less than a quarter of the way to Lake Chad, they met a Tuareg **chieftain**. He and his men seemed friendly and helpful. They offered to guide Tinné all the way to Ghat. This was an oasis town in the heart of the desert. In fact, all the Tuaregs really wanted was Tinné's money.

▲ The Tuaregs are the largest group of people who live in the Sahara. They often wear blue-dyed clothes which leave a blue colour on their skin. They always wear turbans wrapped around their heads and across their faces so that only their eyes show. This protects their faces from the burning Sun and blowing desert sand.

Tinné had brought two iron tanks that were filled with water. Each day, the tanks were loaded carefully on to the camels. The Tuaregs were sure the tanks were full of gold coins. Some days after the Tuaregs joined the caravan, they attacked Tinné's group. The Tuaregs opened the tanks and found only water. They killed the two Dutch bodyguards, and the other people in the caravan ran off. Tinné was left alone and died in the desert. She was only 30 years old.

A traveller in the Lebanon

In the eastern Mediterranean coast are the countries of Turkey, Syria and the Lebanon. A large part of this region is covered by the Syrian Desert. A group of people called the Druze live there. These people kept themselves apart from others and did not welcome strangers. Yet, it was to this area that a British woman, Lady Hester Stanhope, went in the early 1800s.

Lady Hester Stanhope

Lady Hester was born in Britain in 1776. She spent most of her early life with her uncle who was a Prime Minister. She took care of him until his death. Hester had always wanted to travel. At the age of 34, she set out for Turkey with her maid and a doctor. Illness was a European's greatest danger in the eastern Mediterranean. Her travels started in Constantinople, which was the capital of Turkey at that time. There, she risked great danger by not covering her face. Two hundred years ago, all women in Turkey had to wear **veils** over their faces.

◀ Lady Hester Stanhope's journeys in the eastern Mediterranean.

▼ This is Constantinople in Turkey in the 1800s. Lady Hester lived here for two years before she travelled to Egypt. Constantinople is now called Istanbul.

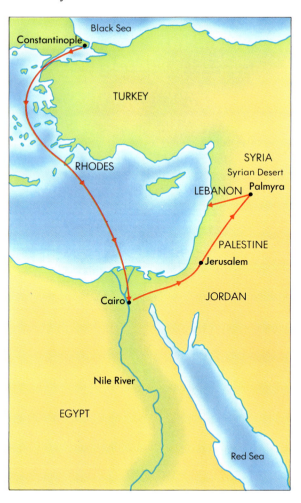

◀ Lady Hester Stanhope wore eastern dress and followed local customs. She was popular with the local people and learned their languages. Lady Hester never returned to Britain. She preferred to stay in the Lebanon.

Shipwrecked

From Constantinople, Hester, her maid and doctor set sail for Egypt. Their ship was caught in a storm. They were lucky to land safely on the island of Rhodes. Hester's clothes were lost with the ship, so she had to wear Turkish dress. She found these loose clothes were better in hot weather than her tight European clothes. After this, she wore that style of clothes for the rest of her life.

From Rhodes, Hester travelled on to Cairo in Egypt. From there, she went to Jerusalem in **Palestine**. Her real aim, however, was to go to the Syrian Desert.

Travels in the desert

By now, Hester had learnt Arabic and other local languages. She wanted to visit the Druze. She was warned that they did not like strangers. They had also never seen a European woman before. However, the Druze liked and admired Hester. They thought she was brave to travel in the desert. They treated her with great respect.

Hester was very proud when she was able to visit the ruined city of Palmyra. She had heard that three British travellers had been attacked while trying to reach the city. So she went dressed up, or **disguised**, as a Bedouin. She was in the company of a Bedouin prince. It was an honour to be taken to Palmyra, even though she had to go in disguise for her own safety.

Hester spent the rest of her life in the Lebanon. She shared all she had with the local people. She gave shelter to poor people in her house on Mount Lebanon. At the age of 63, she died, happy and loved by the people there.

A traveller to Mecca

The Arabian Desert lies east of the Sahara Desert across the Red Sea. Within this area, there are the Muslims' two holy cities of Mecca and Medina.

Each year, thousands of Muslims make a holy journey, or **pilgrimage**, to Mecca. No one but a Muslim can enter the holy city. The only non-Muslims who have been able to get there have gone in disguise. One such man was John Lewis Burckhardt.

John Lewis Burckhardt

Burckhardt was born in Lausanne in Switzerland. He wanted to explore the area around the Niger River and Timbuktu in West Africa. This part of Africa is Muslim, and in those days the people there did not welcome non-Muslims.

In 1809, Burckhardt went to Syria to learn Arabic. He also wanted to learn all he could about the Muslim religion. Then, he planned to go to Cairo. There, he would disguise himself as an Arab. In Cairo, he could join a caravan of **pilgrims** returning from Mecca to West Africa.

In 1812, Burckhardt reached Cairo. He could not find any pilgrims going west, so he set out to visit Dongola in the Sudan. Burckhardt was the first European to reach this area by crossing the Nubian Desert.

On his way back to Cairo, Burkhardt saw the famous temple of Abu Simbel. This is an ancient Egyptian rock temple with four carvings, 20 m high, cut out of the rock.

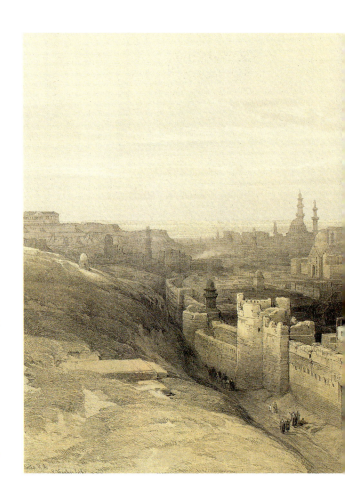

▶ This is an early sketch of Cairo looking west over the Mohammed Ali mosque. It was drawn in 1848. Today, Cairo is the capital of Egypt.

▲ The ancient temple of Abu Simbel was carved out of the mountainside beside the Nile River in southern Egypt. It was built over 3000 years ago by the Pharoah Rameses II. The carved figures which guard the entrance are of the Pharoah himself.

A change of plan

There was still no caravan going to West Africa when Burckhardt returned to Cairo. So he changed his plans and decided to go to Mecca instead. He joined a caravan and went to Shendi, which was a desert market town near Khartoum. There, he joined a group of traders, or **merchants**. They were going to a port on the Red Sea called Suakin. From Suakin, Burckhardt crossed with pilgrims in an open boat to Jeddah, in Arabia. In Jeddah, he met an Egyptian called Mehemet Ali. Mehemet knew about Burckhardt's travels and admired him. He told the local people that Burckhardt was a Muslim. This was not true, but his story made it possible for Burckhardt to enter the holy city of Mecca.

In 1815, Burckhardt got back to Cairo after two and a half years of travelling in the desert. He never managed to go to West Africa as he had first planned. Burckhardt died in Cairo two years later.

▲ Mehemet Ali was a famous soldier who was Master of Egypt in 1805. Here, he entertains some Europeans in his palace in Alexandria.

The Blunts

▲ Lady Anne Blunt dressed as an Arab when she travelled. This made it easier for her to travel among the desert people. These clothes were also more comfortable in the desert heat.

Over 100 years ago, Wilfred Blunt was working in Damascus, in Syria. He was a **diplomat** who worked for the British government. Blunt's wife, Lady Anne, was with him in Syria. They both loved to travel in the Middle East and North Africa.

The Blunts wanted to reach the city of Ha'il in the centre of Arabia. Very few people from Europe had seen this city. It would be a long journey across the Syrian Desert and then across the Nefud Desert in Arabia.

The Blunts hoped they would see Arab horses on their journey. They had a **stud farm** in Britain where they bred racehorses. They wanted to buy some Arab horses and take them back to Britain.

A Bedouin caravan

In 1878, the Blunts set off with a caravan of Bedouin traders. Many of the Bedouin did not want the Blunts to come with them. The Blunts were in constant danger of being attacked. However, a Bedouin chief, or **sheik**, was friendly towards them. He had a lot of power and he was able to protect them.

The Blunts liked to write down an account of all that they saw and heard. Lady Blunt was an artist, and she painted pictures of the desert and the people she met there. Some of the desert people, called the Wahabi, did not like the Blunts making notes. They thought the Blunts might be spies.

▼ This is one of Lady Anne's paintings of a pilgrim camp in Arabia.

Once, the Blunts rode their horses some distance away from the caravan. They got off their horses to take a rest. Then, a group of Wahabi came towards them armed with spears. In a panic, Lady Anne tried to get back to her horse. She twisted her knee and fell. When Wilfred went to help her, the Wahabi seized him. They were about to kill Wilfred when their friend, the sheik, rode up and saved them both.

Buying Arab horses

At last, the Blunts reached Ha'il. There, they met the ruler of the area. He was called Mohammed Ibn Rashid, and he owned many fine Arab racehorses. The horses were smaller than British racehorses, but fast and strong. The Blunts bought some of these horses and sent them back to Britain. Later, the horses were to father many famous racehorses.

The Blunts set out from Ha'il to Bushehr, a port on the north east coast of The Gulf. On their way across the Nefud Desert, they bought more horses to take back to Britain. Finally, they reached Bushehr. They had travelled 3400 km through hot and dry desert country since leaving Syria.

The routes of explorers in the Syrian and Arabian Deserts.

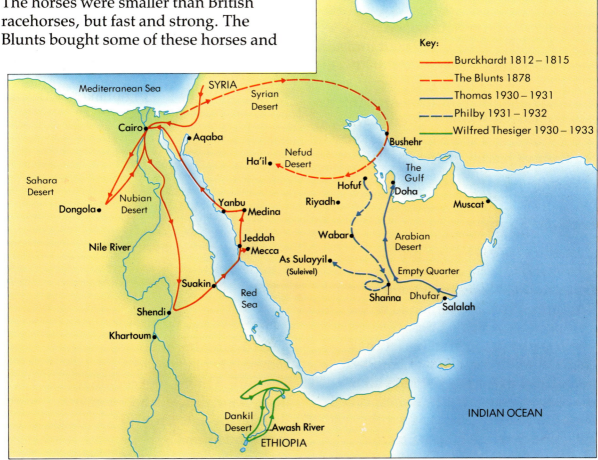

Key:
— Burckhardt 1812 – 1815
--- The Blunts 1878
— Thomas 1930 – 1931
--- Philby 1931 – 1932
— Wilfred Thesiger 1930 – 1933

19

The Empty Quarter

By 1930, most of the world's deserts had been crossed and mapped. In Saudi Arabia, there was one desert which no European had crossed. This is known as the Empty Quarter. It is a good name for an area of 400 000 sq km of **sand dunes**. Sometimes, these hills of sand are over 100 m high. The Empty Quarter is burning hot during the day. At night, it is freezing cold. There are very few water-holes, and so people do not stay in the Empty Quarter for long.

▲ The sand dunes in the Empty Quarter can be very high. The wind moves the sand dunes, so that the landscape can look different each day.

▼ Bertram Thomas seated on the camel, with his guides in Oman in 1930. He was the first European to cross the Empty Quarter.

Bertram Thomas

Bertram Thomas was a British diplomat. He had been working and exploring in Muscat and Oman on The Gulf since 1924. He wanted to be the first European to cross the Empty Quarter. Thomas planned to start his journey from the south coast. It was hard to persuade the Bedouin to guide him across the desert. At last, a sheik called Salih bin Yakut, agreed to go with Thomas across the Empty Quarter.

In December 1930, Thomas set off with Sheik Yakut, his Bedouins and their camels. He planned to reach Doha on The Gulf. On the journey, they saw many sand dunes, and Thomas admired their shape and size. They also had to face **sandstorms**.

During these sandstorms, the wind blew the sand into their eyes, noses and mouths. It was hard to travel when the wind was very strong.

As Thomas and the Bedouins got close to Doha, the Bedouins sang songs to their camels about water. The thirsty camels pricked up their ears and began to walk more quickly. They reached Doha on 5 February 1931. Thomas had crossed the Empty Quarter.

The city destroyed by God

Another man from Britain, called Harry Philby, also wanted to cross the Empty Quarter. He wanted to find the ancient city of Wabar. The desert people thought God had 'destroyed' the city because the people there were wicked. Arab travellers said that only a large lump of metal now stood where the city had been.

On 7 January 1932, Philby set out from Hofuf in the north with some Bedouins. He went south into the centre of the desert. There, he found that Wabar was really two large holes, or **craters**, in the ground. They were about 100 m wide and 10 m deep. They had been made by **meteorites**. Meteorites are pieces of rock which travel in space. Sometimes, they hit the Earth.

In one of the craters, Philby found a large piece of iron. It was the remains of the meteorite. Perhaps this was the large lump of metal which the desert people believed was once the wicked city of Wabar.

Philby moved south across the Empty Quarter. Then, he turned west and at last reached the Suleivel Oasis. It was 11 March 1932. He had crossed the Empty Quarter. After Philby's journey, no European crossed the Empty Quarter again for 14 years.

▼ Harry Philby photographed with the Bedouin tribesmen who travelled with him.

The man who loved the desert

People explored deserts for many reasons. Wilfred Thesiger went into the deserts because he admired the people who lived there. He liked their way of life. Later in his life, he made two journeys in the Empty Quarter between 1946 and 1948. He wrote about his journeys in a book called *Arabian Sands*. He praised the courage and kindness of the people in that area.

Wilfred Thesiger

Thesiger was born in Ethiopia in Africa. He made his first journey into the desert in 1930. He spent a month in the Danakil. This is a harsh area in northern Ethiopia. It is one of the hottest places in the world. Thesiger travelled on foot, and at night he slept under the stars. He was alone with no one to help him if he fell ill. He was often tired, thirsty and afraid. In spite of this, he was happy. He had found the magic and mystery of the desert.

▲Wilfred Thesiger during his crossing of the Empty Quarter.

Thesiger met the people who lived in the desert. They were armed with ancient guns, or **muskets**. They carried their guns across the back of their necks, and hooked their arms up and over the guns. This helped them to sweat less in the fierce heat and to breathe more easily. You can still see people carrying guns like this in Ethiopia today.

▲ This is the salt lake in the Danakil which Wilfred Thesiger found to be very barren and very hot.

A mystery solved

Three years after his first trip, Thesiger went back to the Danakil. He managed to persuade the local ruler, or **sultan**, to let him explore an area no European had been allowed to travel through before. This area was around the Awash River. This river was a mystery. It did not seem to flow into the sea as other rivers do.

◀ Wilfred Thesiger sitting in the middle of four Bedouin people. They are all armed with muskets.

Thesiger followed the course of the Awash and found it ended in a large salt lake. On this lake, he saw red plant matter floating on the surface. Thesiger said this **algae** looked like dried blood. The whole lake looked dismal and gloomy. The only wildlife he saw were small **wading birds** and a few very small, yellow-eyed crocodiles.

Thesiger was lucky to survive his trips through the barren Danakil. The people there were well-known for their violent way of life. Even well-armed caravans of traders had been killed. This was the first of the desert areas Thesiger was to explore. His desert travels went on all through his life.

The Gobi Desert

A Chinese traveller

The Gobi Desert in Asia is one of the largest desert areas in the world. It stretches across most of Mongolia and the north of China. It is shut in by mountains to the north, south and west. In summer, it is very hot during the day, but at night the temperature falls steeply. In winter, it is very cold and there are snowstorms, or **blizzards**.

There is very little water in the Gobi Desert. It rains very little and there are just a few streams and no big rivers at all. Most of the area is bare rock. In summer, a little coarse grass and some thorny bushes grow there. In some places, there is just enough grass to feed a few sheep, horses and camels.

About 1300 years ago, a young Chinese priest, or **monk**, set out from China to travel to India. His name was Hsuan-Tsang and he was 19 years old. He wanted to find out more about his religion of **Buddhism** from the Buddhist monks in India. The ruler of China had told Hsuan-Tsang not to go to India. He was angry when he heard that the young monk had left with some friends and a guide.

Ahead of Hsuan-Tsang lay the Gobi Desert. His friends and the guide all turned back. They did not want to risk crossing the desert, so Hsuan-Tsang went on alone. He had no maps or guide to show him the way. He rode a horse which had crossed the Gobi Desert many times before.

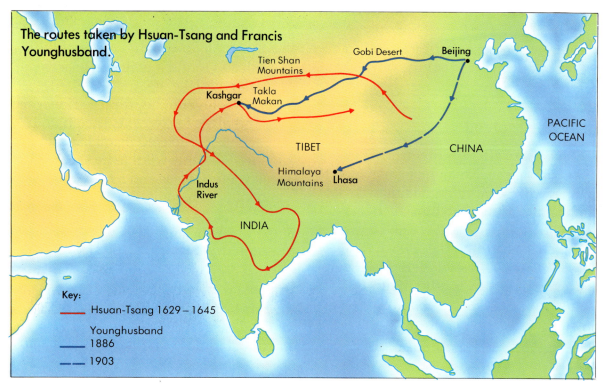

The routes taken by Hsuan-Tsang and Francis Younghusband.

Key:
— Hsuan-Tsang 1629–1645
— Younghusband 1886
--- 1903

▲ This is a cave painting of Hsuan-Tsang. It was painted by Buddhist monks.

Across the Gobi Desert

Hsuan-Tsang tried to follow the tracks of camels and other animals. He was in danger of losing the way. Several times he nearly died of thirst. Once, his **water-skin** dropped and burst. He went for five days without water before he was saved by a sudden shower of rain. Once, he was saved by his horse. It refused to go the way Hsuan-Tsang wanted and took him to a pool of water. Hsuan-Tsang said the pool was 'as sweet and bright as a mirror'. Later, he wrote about the Gobi Desert. He said, 'There are no birds overhead, and no beasts below. There is neither water nor herbs to be found'.

Sixteen years later, Hsuan-Tsang went back to China across the desert. He had spent many years in Tibet, India and **Ceylon**, living with Buddhist monks and travelling about. The ruler of China forgave Hsuan-Tsang and asked him to write books about his journeys.

▲ This picture was painted over 1000 years ago. It shows Hsuan-Tsang returning from his travels in India on an elephant.

The forbidden city

About 100 years ago, the British Empire ruled most of India. The British feared that the Russians would try to move into Afghanistan and Tibet which are to the north of India. Both the British and the Russians had tried to get to the city of Lhasa, the capital of Tibet. This was the home of the ruler, the Dalai Lama. It was hard for **foreigners** from other lands to reach the Dalai Lama's city. The local people attacked strangers. Also, the city was in a **remote** place. To the south lay the Himalaya Mountains. To the north east lay the Gobi Desert.

▲ The Gobi Desert is treeless and rocky. It is the coldest, most northern desert in the world.

Francis Younghusband

Francis Younghusband was an officer in the British Army. In 1886, he was sent to Beijing, in China. There, the army allowed him to cross overland from Beijing to Kashgar. Kashgar was close to the Pamir Mountains. It was a journey of about 3200 km, and it would take him across the Gobi Desert.

On 4 April 1886, Younghusband set out from Beijing with only a guide, a Chinese cook and eight camels. In two weeks, they reached a small town on the

◀ The Dalai Lama was the supreme ruler of Tibet. He was worshipped as a god and thought to be holy. This is the 13th Dalai Lama, photographed when he was 24.

▲ Francis Younghusband and his soldiers marching past one of the Tibetan fortresses.

edge of the Gobi Desert. There, they hired five more camels and a guide who knew the way across the desert.

In order to avoid the hottest part of the day, Younghusband and his group began their journey at three in the afternoon. They rode their camels until midnight, often using the stars to guide them. The air was very dry and had some strange effects. The group's blankets crackled and sparked with electricity when they spread them out!

Younghusband and his men said that they saw only a few brown bushes and no grass. They only found water in rough water-holes which people in other caravans had dug before them. The journey across the Gobi Desert took 70 days. At the end, the group rode for 28 hours to cover the last 112 km to an oasis.

After Younghusband left the Gobi Desert, he had another 1400 km to travel before he reached Kashgar. He had to cross another desert called the Takla Makan which is south of the Tien Shan Mountains. From there, he crossed to Kashgar.

Journey to Tibet

Younghusband was one of the few people to have crossed central Asia from Beijing to Kashgar. It was because of this journey that the British decided to send him into Tibet to find the city of Lhasa. In 1903, Younghusband set out with **porters**, pack animals and 3000 soldiers. Among the animals were two zebrules, which were a cross between a zebra and a mule. The journey was difficult and full of danger. Many of the animals died, and there were constant attacks by the local people. At last, Younghusband and his men arrived in Lhasa.

The Australian Desert

While the Sahara Desert was being explored and mapped, people began to explore the vast empty areas of Australia. People had settled along the coastal regions. Most of them lived in the south east of Australia where there was more rain. There, they built the towns of Sydney, Adelaide and Melbourne. The inland region of the continent was largely unknown up to 150 years ago.

Charles Sturt

Charles Sturt was one of the early explorers of the inland areas of Australia. He had watched birds flying north, so he thought there must be water inland. In 1844, he set out to explore central Australia. He wanted to find places where people could make their homes. Sturt went with 15 men, 11 horses, 200 sheep and 30 bullocks. The group went up the Murray and Darling Rivers as far as they could. Then, they went north across the Main Barrier Range. In this area, there were only a few water-holes.

It was summer, and the heat rose to amost 50°C. Matches caught fire, and the wool on the sheep stopped growing! The men and animals were saved when Sturt found a large water-hole near Malparinka on 27 January 1845. There, they dug shelters under the ground and waited for the cooler weather. Then, Sturt tried to move further inland again.

▲ Alice Springs is in the Northern Territory, and is right in the middle of Australia. This is the type of desert country around the town of Alice Springs that many of the early Australian explorers travelled through.

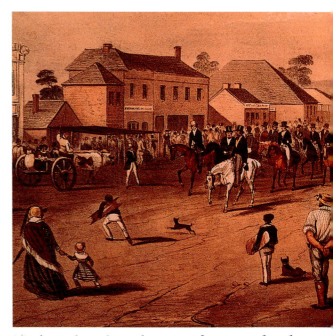

He found nothing but a rocky **wasteland**. This is now called the Sturt Desert. There were no water-holes so the men had to turn back.

John Stuart

More people started to settle in Australia. The South Australian government wanted to lay a **cable** line across the continent. A reward of £2000 was offered to anyone who could cross the continent from south to north.

John Stuart, who had travelled with Sturt, wanted to collect the reward. He set out from Adelaide with two other men. They crossed the Macdonnell Range in the centre of Australia and reached what is now called Mount Stuart. There, they were forced to turn back because of lack of water, and illness. The men had got within 480 km of the **Gulf** of Carpentaria in north east Australia.

▲ John Stuart was born in Scotland and had travelled with Charles Sturt into the interior of Australia. In 1861, he reached Darling after travelling from Adelaide on the south coast.

When Stuart got back to Adelaide, the government were pleased with his effort. They gave him money for another expedition. In January 1861, Stuart set off again with 13 men and 49 horses. They were able to get just a little further than Stuart had on his previous journey.

On a later journey, Stuart did reach the north coast. In July 1862, he saw the Indian Ocean at the mouth of the Mary River on Van Diemen Gulf. He was very pleased, but his health had suffered because of the difficult journey. He died four years later.

▲ The departure of the British explorer, Captain Charles Sturt, on his expedition into the interior of Australia in 1844. Earlier, he had explored the Darling River and the Lower Murray River.

The race from south to north

Key:
— Sturt 1844 – 1846
— — Stuart 1858 – 1862
— Burke and Wills 1860 – 1861
  Giles
— 1873
— — 1876

Van Diemen Gulf
Gulf of Carpentaria
Great Sandy Desert
INDIAN OCEAN
Mount Stuart
Macdonnell Range
Gibson Desert
Alice Springs
Mount Destruction
Ayers Rock
Great Victoria Desert
Ayers Range
Simpson Desert
Cooper's Creek
Sturt Desert
Lake Eyre
Main Barrier Range
Malparinka
Darling River
Mount Hopeless
Menindee
Sydney
Perth
Adelaide
Murray River
Melbourne

▲ The routes taken by the early Australian explorers. The four major deserts in Australia are the Simpson, the Gibson, the Great Sandy and the Great Victoria. The cover about one-third of the land area.

The attempt to cross Australia from south to north became a race. The state of Victoria set up an expedition. They chose a man called Robert Burke to lead it. The problem was that Burke knew nothing about travelling in the desert.

On 20 August 1860, Burke and his group set off from Melbourne towards the north. Burke went with 18 men, some camels, horses and 21 tonnes of dried food and supplies. They pushed on towards Menindee, which was 640 km north of Melbourne. They covered 32 km a day. Burke gave an order that food should be left behind to help them travel faster. He even left behind the lime juice. This was a bad mistake. It was needed to keep the men healthy. The lime juice contained **vitamin C**. This would protect the men from a disease called **scurvy**.

It soon became clear that Burke could not gain the trust of many of his men. Before they even reached Menindee, nine men had left Burke. Among them were the doctor and the second in command, George Landells, who had argued with Burke.

▲ The start of the Robert Burke and William Wills expedition in Melbourne in 1860. The explorers succeeded in crossing the continent but died of starvation on the return journey.

Towards Cooper's Creek

At Menindee, Burke chose a local man, William Wright, to wait for the rest of the supplies. These were being sent behind them. Wright was to join Burke with these supplies 640 km further north at Cooper's **Creek**. Burke went on through the dry and rocky Sturt Desert to Cooper's Creek. He took seven men, some camels and horses with him. There, they set up a camp and waited for Wright to join them. There was water to drink and a little shade under the trees to protect them from the fierce sun. There were, however, hundreds of rats, so they had to hang their food in the trees. The men waited for five weeks, but Wright did not appear.

To the Gulf of Carpentaria

Burke could not wait any longer. He left a man called William Brahé and three others behind to wait for Wright. They were to guard the food they had left in the trees at the camp. Burke chose three men, William Wills, John King and Charles Gray to go with him on the last stretch of the journey. They had three months' supply of food with them, some camels, and a pony called Billy. After travelling north for 1120 km, they entered a damp, soft, **swampy** area which the camels could not get through. Burke left the camels with Gray and King, and he set off on foot with Wills to travel the last 48 km to the coast. At last, in February 1861, they got to the sea. They were the first men to cross Australia from south to north. They had made a journey of over 2400 km.

31

A hard journey back

Burke and Wills had now crossed the continent. They were worried as they turned back to Cooper's Creek. It had taken them two months to get to the sea from Cooper's Creek. They had a long journey ahead of them, and they only had one month's supply of food left.

Burke and Wills met Gray and King, with their pony Billy, as they made their way back across the swamp. Burke told the men they would have to cut their daily **rations** of food by half. For ten days, they were slowed down by heavy rainstorms. It took over a month for the men to cross the swamp into the desert. They were becoming weaker and weaker from lack of food. Gray could not walk any longer, and finally he died from weakness and hunger. After four months, Burke, Wills and King reached Cooper's Creek.

At Cooper's Creek

Brahé and the three other men had waited for Burke at Cooper's Creek. Brahé had had a hard time at the camp. The rats had gone on trying to eat the food, and the men were also weak from fever. There was also no sign of Wright, who was supposed to be coming with supplies of food. Burke had said he would be back in three months. After nearly four months of waiting, Brahé decided to go south to find Wright. He left a supply of food, and a note for Burke in case he returned.

▲ Cooper's Creek was made into a permanent camp for Burke and his men. More food and more men were supposed to be sent to Cooper's Creek but they arrived too late.

About seven hours after Brahé left, Burke got back to Cooper's Creek. He found the note and the food that Brahé had left. Now, he had to decide what was the best thing to do. He could try to catch up with Brahé, or he could try to get across the desert to a cattle station at Mount Hopeless. Burke decided to go to the cattle station, which was 320 km away. He hid a small supply of food, and then left a note for Brahé to say where he had gone.

▲ Robert Burke, William Wills and John King tried to reach Mount Hopeless to find help. They ran out of water and food and had to turn back to Cooper's Creek.

Brahé meets Wright

Brahé went south and met Wright. Together, they went back to Cooper's Creek to find Burke. When they got there, they found no sign of Burke and his men. Brahé and Wright did not notice that the food Brahé had left had been taken. They also did not see the note Burke had left behind about his plan to find help at Mount Hopeless. They were sure that Burke and his men were lost forever.

▲ John King was to be the only survivor of the expedition.

Back to Cooper's Creek

Burke, Wills and King could not get as far as Mount Hopeless. They could find no water on the way, and they had no food left. Burke decided to turn back to Cooper's Creek. There, they could find water, and the food which they had hidden. By this time, the men were very weak from hunger and thirst. Sometimes, they were able to shoot a crow. At other times, they lived on the seeds of desert plants. Once, they met some local people called **Aborigines**. The Aborigines have lived in the desert for thousands of years. They have learned how to find enough food to eat and water to drink. Burke was afraid of them and he fired his pistol into the air to keep them away. At last, the three men struggled back to Cooper's Creek.

Help from the Aborigines

Burke knew he had to find help. There was not much food left at Cooper's Creek so he set off again with King. They left Wills behind because he was so weak. Now that Wills was alone, the Aborigines came to help him. They shared their food with him. After a short time, Wills regained some of his strength. He set out again, and caught up with Burke and King. The small amount of food they had taken with them was gone. They were living on desert plants and seeds.

▲ These water-holding frogs provide water for the Aborigines. The frogs can survive a dry period in the desert of up to a year. They store water in their bodies and then bury themselves in mud. The frogs come up to the surface again when the rain comes.

At last, Burke decided to ask the Aborigines for help. By this time, however, the Aborigines had left their camp to go **walkabout**. Wills was now so weak that he could not stand up, so Burke and King left him again at the camp. They set off to try to find the Aborigines.

▲ John King sitting by the body of Robert Burke. It had been a successful expedition because they had reached the Gulf of Carpentaria in the north. The expedition, however, had a tragic ending.

A tragic ending

Burke and King failed to find the Aborigines. Burke was now so weak he could not carry on. He died on 30 June. As King stood by his dead friend, he felt he was being watched. There were several weeping Aborigines behind him. They took King back to their camp to find Wills. When they got there, they found Wills had also died.

The Aborigines fed and looked after King at their camp. About 11 weeks later, a rescue party arrived. The rescue party was led by Alfred Howitt of Melbourne. It was one of the four groups who had been sent out to look for Burke and his men. King was alive, but by this time he was so thin that he could hardly move. The Aborigines had tried to feed him, but he was already too weak when they found him. The rescue party took him back to safety, but he died two years later from ill health.

▲ Eventually, the bodies of Robert Burke and William Wills were found. They were taken back to Melbourne and given a large funeral.

Across Australia

The continent had been crossed from south to north. Now, the race was on to find a route from central Australia to the west coast.

Ernest Giles

Ernest Giles first tried to cross from central Australia to the west coast in 1872. His first attempt failed. In 1873, he set out from Adelaide again. With Alf Gibson and two others, he started his journey west from Lake Eyre. This place is south east of the town of Alice Springs.

▲ Ernest Giles was born in Britain in 1835. He became a famous Australian explorer, and set out on four expeditions to the west coast between 1872 and 1876.

At first, the men travelled through a grassy valley which was full of flowers and birds. Then, they went on to Ayers Range, south of the Macdonnell Range. These hills were 'huge, red, rounded blocks of stone'. The only problem for the men was an attack by Aborigines which they were able to drive off. The Aborigines may have attacked Giles because he and his men were getting too close to Ayers Rock. This is a holy place for the Aborigines.

Finding a route

The country had grown drier and drier as Giles and his men got closer to Ayers Rock. They made a camp past Ayers Rock in a place where there was water.

From the camp, Giles went on alone to find a good route. He rode for about 140 km but he was forced to turn back by the heat and lack of water. He did not realize when he turned back that he was only 18 km from water.

▲ Ernest Giles had to drink from any water-holes he could find during his trips. Sometimes, the water was pure, often it was stagnant. The stagnant water would have made him ill.

It was almost the end of December when Giles returned to the camp. On Christmas Day, the men were attacked by Aborigines. Giles fired his rifle and they ran away. Giles led his men north west. On the route they found a pool deep enough to bathe in. After that, they found no more water and their horses died. On reaching what Giles named the Mountain of Destruction, the men turned back to Ayers Rock.

▲ Ayers Rock in the Northern Territory is 2.4 km long and 300 m high. It contains many small caves with rock paintings. These were made long ago by Aborigine artists.

The last attempts

Giles set out again to find a route from Adelaide to the west coast. He took Alf Gibson, four horses, some food and 180 litres of water with him. After travelling 96 km, they set two horses free to make their own way back. They also hung 45 litres of water in a tree for the return journey. The water was stored in small barrels, or **kegs**. They rode on for another 180 km. This was as far as they could risk travelling without finding water. On the way back, one of the horses collapsed. Giles sent Gibson on ahead with the one remaining horse. Giles travelled on foot. He got back to the kegs of water and then he made the journey back alone to the camp at Ayers Rock. Gibson did not come back, and Giles never saw him again.

In 1876, Giles set out again from Adelaide, but this time he took camels with him instead of horses. He reached Perth on the west coast. He then returned to Adelaide and became the first man to make the crossing in both directions.

The North American Desert

The south west of the United States is not thought of by most people today as a desert, like the Sahara Desert or the Gobi Desert. There are many areas that are very hot and very dry, but there are also grasslands, or **prairies**, to the north. The first explorers called all of this area the Great American Desert. This was because they could not find enough water to farm the land or to live there safely.

The two expeditions

The Spanish settlers from Mexico were the first to explore the south west of America. In 1539, travellers told stories about the Seven Cities of Cibola. These cities were said to be full of gold. The Spaniards planned two expeditions. One group was to go up the west coast by sea with several small ships. It was led by Pedro Alarcón. He did not find any gold, but he did map the Gulf of California.

The other group would go by land with 300 men and 1000 horses. This group was led by Francisco Coronado.

▶ Francisco Coronado came from Mexico. In 1540, he led an expedition into the American south west in search of the Seven Cities of Cibola. American Indians had said that these cities were rich in gold, but Coronado never found any.

▲ The routes of Francisco Coronado, Jedediah Smith and John Charles Frémont.

Coronado's journey

In 1540, Coronado's men rode northwards. They went up the Sonora Valley into southern Arizona. His group travelled over 2400 km of mountains and deserts. Coronado wrote that they saw 'grey lions and leopards'. These may have been cougars and wild cats. When at last they found Cibola, there were no golden cities. There were only the villages of the Zuni people. These people did not welcome strangers and their attacks slowed down the men as they moved north.

▼ The largest herds of elk now live in Yellowstone National Park. In Coronado's time, they roamed across America.

Coronado's group reached the Grand Canyon. They spent the winter in a village in the Santa Fé Mountains. There, they were told of gold further north. In the early spring, the group moved on. They travelled across the Great Plains which were full of elk and deer. From there, they moved on into Texas and found herds of buffalo. The group could find no gold.

In a last attempt, Coronado led a group into Oklahoma. The Spaniards saw the good black soil but they wanted gold and not farming land. Coronado then returned to Mexico. His group had not found any gold to the north.

Jedediah Smith

Three hundred years passed before new settlers began to explore the south west of the United States. The first American to travel in the western desert was Jedediah Smith. Smith was a **fur trapper**, and he had spent three years in the forests near the Rocky Mountains.

In the early 1800s, California was part of Mexico. The only way to the west coast was along the Columbia River to the north. There were no routes through the Rockies.

▲ Jedediah Smith was looking for fur trade routes across the Rocky Mountains. He made the first land exploration of Oregon and Washington. He was killed in 1831 on the Santa Fé trail.

▲ A trapper with his horse and furs in the Rocky Mountains.

A journey to the south west

In August 1826, Smith and a group of trappers left a town called Rendezvous near Great Salt Lake. They were looking for beaver in an area south west of Salt Lake. The group crossed southern Nevada. On their route, they could not find any beaver nor any water. The men struggled on, and to their surprise they came across a green valley. This was the land of the Mojave people. These people fed and cared for Smith and his men. They sold horses to Smith and guided his group across the dry Mojave Desert. At last on 27 November, Smith and his men arrived at the Mission of San Gabriel.

The return to Rendezvous

The Mexican governor of California heard about Smith's journey. He was worried that Americans would find a route overland to California.

Smith wrote to him to explain the reason for his journey. The governor told him to go back across the Mojave Desert. Smith agreed but when he got 80 km inland, he turned north.

After travelling about 500 km, the group came to the American River area. At last, they found hundreds of beaver. It was now May 1827. Smith split his group. He would go ahead with two men and seven horses. The others would wait for his return.

Smith and his men set off over the Sierra Nevada. It was freezing cold as they climbed over the mountains. Four of the horses died, and the men were weak from cold and hunger.

At last, the men reached the grasslands and water. They had travelled over 3000 km and had found a way through to California.

Smith went back to California to find his men. They all returned safely to Rendezvous. In the next 100 years, millions of people moved into California. Few people used Smith's route through the mountains because the route was not good for wagons. However, Smith's maps and writings about his travels helped others to settle in that area.

▲ The Grand Canyon in the Arizona Desert with the Colorado River at the bottom. The first desert explorers who saw the Canyon were Francisco Coronado and his men in 1540.

Explorers and settlers

About 150 years ago, Americans began to move west to look for new land to farm and to settle in. The explorers had opened up new routes across the mountains and the deserts. The farmers and traders followed them when they heard there were passable trails and good land to be found. The United States government sent people to find this new land. Many of the explorers who were sent were in the army and knew about making maps. One of these men was John Charles Frémont.

▲ A pioneer wagon train. The covered wagon was a home for the pioneers and it carried all their belongings. The journey across the Great American Desert was over 3000 km, and it could take up to three months. It was a dangerous and rough journey. The early pioneers thought the desert land was poor. Later, people realized that it was good farm land.

Frémont the Pathfinder

In 1842, Frémont went on his first journey to the Rockies. He mapped the area around Great Salt Lake. A year later, Frémont went on a second journey. Kit Carson, the well-known mountain man, went with him. They mapped the area around the mouth of the Columbia River. Then, the group went south and crossed the Sierra Nevada Mountains in winter. The snow made this a very hard journey. One man went mad and a number of men had **snow blindness**. They could not see where to put their feet safely to make the next step. When the men got through to California, they mapped the Sacramento Valley. The group went south through the San Joaquin Valley and returned eastwards through Colorado.

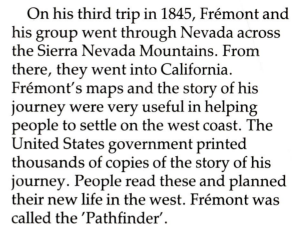

▲ John Charles Frémont explored and mapped much of the area between the Rocky Mountains and the Pacific Ocean. He helped produce the first scientific maps of the American West. He once stood for President of the United States, but he lost.

On his third trip in 1845, Frémont and his group went through Nevada across the Sierra Nevada Mountains. From there, they went into California. Frémont's maps and the story of his journey were very useful in helping people to settle on the west coast. The United States government printed thousands of copies of the story of his journey. People read these and planned their new life in the west. Frémont was called the 'Pathfinder'.

Frémont as governor

In 1846, the United States Army fought the Mexicans. They won California for the Americans. Frémont knew the routes across the Sierra Nevada into California. He helped with the **conquest** of this new state. He then became the first governor of California. It was men like Frémont who showed the Americans that much of the area they called the Great American Desert was good land. People could settle and farm there.

The end of an age

What desert areas are left for pathfinders to explore? Today, we have strong trucks and planes to cross the deserts in. Most of these areas are well mapped. The true explorers of the future will look to the Moon and planets for new deserts to map and explore.

◀ Deserts are no longer such difficult places to cross. Today, we have cars, planes and maps. The early explorers had to rely on horses, camels, the desert people and their own courage.

Quiz

How much can you remember about this book? Try this quiz and use your index and glossary to help you check your answers.

1. Here are some names of famous desert explorers with the letters mixed up. Try to find the correct names.

   a) MITHS, b) SLIGE, c) SWILL, d) DORNOCOA, e) STRUT, f) KURBE, g) GRISETHE, h) HOTESPAN

2. Can you guess what this sentence says in full?
   'There are _____ birds _____, and no _____ below. There is _____ water nor _____ to be found'.
   Clue: A Chinese monk said this about the Gobi Desert.

3. Put the following events in the order they took place:
   a) Burke and Wills make the south to north crossing of Australia.
   b) Bertram Thomas crosses the Empty Quarter.
   c) Younghusband enters the city of Lhasa.
   d) Lady Hester Stanhope visits Palmyra.
   e) A Chinese monk sets out alone across the Gobi Desert.

4. Match the descriptions given in (a) to (f) with the words numbered (1) to (6) below them.

   a) People who move around a great deal in the desert
   b) A group of traders travelling with camels in the desert
   c) A holy city of Islam
   d) The largest desert in Africa
   e) Hills of sand in the desert
   f) Water-holes in the desert

   1) the Sahara
   2) oases
   3) caravan
   4) nomads
   5) dunes
   6) Mecca

5. Complete the following sentences with (a), (b), (c) or (d).
   1) Hsuan-Tsang crossed the
      a) Sahara Desert.
      b) Arabian Desert.
      c) Gobi Desert.
      d) Sturt Desert.

   2) Which of these desert travellers crossed the Empty Quarter?
      a) Robert Burke
      b) Harry Philby
      c) Francis Younghusband
      d) Alexandrine Tinné

   3) Kano is a city in
      a) Australia.
      b) America.
      c) Asia.
      d) Africa.

   4) Cooper's Creek is in
      a) Africa.
      b) Arabia.

c) Australia.
d) the United States.

5) Jedediah Smith was a
  a) soldier.
  b) fur trapper.
  c) diplomat
  d) sailor.

6. How many desert explorers can you find with names beginning with B, S or T?

7. Which desert would you be in if
  a) it stretched from the Red Sea to the Gulf?
  b) it was the largest in the world?
  c) the Druze lived there?
  d) you were in Asia and shut in by mountains to the north, south and west?
  e) you were close to the mission of San Gabriel?

8. Who or what
  a) is 'The Great Traveller of Islam'?
  b) is used to make gunpowder?
  c) went to Kano with a dyed face?
  d) carried two iron tanks filled with water in the Sahara?
  e) entered Mecca with an Egyptian called Mehemet Ali?

9. Are these statements true or false?
  a) The Blunts bought horses in the Gobi Desert.
  b) Burckhardt travelled in West Africa.
  c) A holy journey is called a pilgrimage.
  d) Frémont became the first military governor of California.
  e) John Stuart crossed Australia from south to north.

Answers

1. a) SMITH, b) GILES, c) WILLS, d) CORONADO, e) STURT, f) BURKE, g) THESIGER, h) STANHOPE

2. 'There are no birds overhead, and no beasts below. There is neither water nor herbs to be found'.

3. (e), (d), (a), (c), (b)

4. (a) 4, (b) 3, (c) 6, (d) 1, (e) 5, (f) 2

5. 1 (c), 2 (b), 3 (d), 4 (c), 5 (b)

6. Battuta, Barth, Burckhardt, Blunts, Burke, Braké, Stanhope, Sturt, Stuart Smith, Thesiger, Tinné, Thomas

7. a) the Arabian Desert
b) the Sahara Desert
c) the Syrian Desert
d) the Gobi Desert
e) the Mojave Desert

8. a) Battuta
b) saltpetre
c) Barth
d) Tinné
e) Burckhardt

9. a) True, b) False, c) True, d) True, e) True

Glossary

Aborigine: the name given to the first people to live in Australia. It comes from a Latin word meaning 'from the beginning'

algae: very simple plants. Algae have no leaves, roots or stems. Most algae are found in water

barren: describes land which cannot produce crops

base: a place from which an organization or expedition works and keeps its main supplies

blizzard: a snowstorm blown by a very strong, cold wind

Buddhism: the religion of the Buddhists who follow the teachings of Buddha

cable line: a bundle of insulated wires which are used to carry telegraph messages

caravan: a group of people and their camels travelling across the desert

Ceylon: an island in the Indian Ocean, off the south east coast of India. The name of the island was changed to Sri Lanka in 1972

chieftain: the leader or ruler of a group of people or a tribe

continent: a large mass of land, usually including many countries. The Earth is divided into seven continents

conquest: the act of overcoming or defeating an enemy

crater: a bowl-shaped hollow made by an explosion, or a large object from space

creek: a stream

desert: an area of dry land which has little or no rainfall. Plants cannot easily grow in deserts

diplomat: a person who represents his or her own country in another country

disguise: to change the appearance of someone by wearing different clothes

expedition: an organized journey which is made for a special purpose. Explorers went on expeditions to find out about other lands

foreigner: a person who belongs to another country

fur trapper: a person who sets traps to catch animals with fur, such as rabbit, mink, or beaver

gulf: a part of the ocean or sea which goes into the land in a wide deep bay or channel

Islam: the religion of the Muslims which follows the teaching of Muhammad

keg: a small barrel

merchant: a person who buys and sells goods, often dealing with other countries

meteorite: a piece of rock or metal from space which has crashed into the Earth's surface

monk: a man who lives in a religious group

millet: a type of grass which produces seeds that can be eaten

musket: a type of long-barrelled gun fired from the shoulder. Muskets were used in the 1700s and 1800s by soldiers and hunters

Muslim: someone who follows the religion of Islam and the teachings of Muhammad

nomad: someone who moves about from place to place in search of food or to find grass for animals. Nomads do not make their homes in one particular place

oasis: a place in the desert where underground water comes to the surface and plants can grow

Palestine: the area between the Jordan River and the Mediterranean Sea

peak: the top of a mountain

pilgrim: a person who makes a journey to a holy or special place

pilgrimage: a journey to a holy or special place

porter: a person who is hired to carry goods

prairie: a large, open area of grassland without trees. The grasslands of North America are called prairies

preserve: to stop something from rotting or spoiling. Today, food is often preserved by cooking or freezing

ration: an amount of food shared out among people

region: a district or an area

remote: describes something which is far away from other places. A remote island is a long way from other land

route: the way to get from one place to another. Routes are shown on maps and plans

saltpetre: a white powder used for making gunpowder or fireworks. Saltpetre is also used as a fertilizer

sand dune: a hill of sand built by the wind

sandstorm: a desert wind storm which carries along clouds of sand

scurvy: a disease caused by the lack of vitamin C. This disease leads to bleeding of the gums and damage to the teeth and bones of the body

sheik: the head man or leader of a group of Arabic people

snow blindness: a condition of the eyes which makes them red and very sensitive to light. Snow blindness is caused by the eyes receiving too much reflected light from the ice and snow

stud farm: a place where horses are kept for breeding purposes

sultan: the ruler of a Muslim country

supplies: the food, fuel or equipment needed for an expedition

swampy: describes wet, soft ground

temperature: the measure of how hot or cold something is. Thermometers are used to measure temperatures

trader: someone who does business by buying and selling goods

treasure: a collection of precious metals and stones, like gold and diamonds

veil: a piece of fabric worn across the bottom half of the face. Veils were often worn to protect the face from sun and dust

vitamin C: a substance which is found in foods such as fresh vegetables and fruit. Vitamin C is essential for good health

wading bird: a type of long legged bird that lives near water

walkabout: one of the periodic journeys made by Aborigines into the bush in Australia

wasteland: an area not lived in or used for any purpose

water-skin: a bag made out of an animal skin. Water-skins were used for carrying water across deserts

Index